STILL LIFE WITH PIPE, 1914-15
Oil, 21¾" x 39"
Pierre Lévy Collection, Troyes

PORTRAIT OF MOÏSE KISLING, undated
Oil, 39" x 27¼"
Philadelphia Museum of Art

PORTRAIT OF A NURSE, ca. 1916
Oil, 25½" x 19½"
Los Angeles County Museum of Art

LANDSCAPE WITH HOUSE, undated
Oil, 17½" x 20"
Yale University Art Gallery

12

FALLEN TREE, 1922-23
Oil, 23¾" x 32"
Walter - Guillaume Collection, Paris

THE WHITE HOUSE, 1919 Oil, 27½" x 23" Walter - Guillaume Collection, Paris

for Soutine was a leg injury, fifteen days in the hospital, and, by order of the justice of the peace, a compensation payment of twenty five rubles by his attackers.

After his family had taken its share of this compensation payment, Chaim had enough money left to take him to Vilna, a larger city in Lithuania. Here, after failing the entrance examination, pleading despairingly with Professor Rebakoff, and successfully softening the heart of the director, one Troutnioff, he was accepted into art school.

The strengthening of his friendship with Kikoïne dates from this period. This young man, from the same region, had been a friend of Soutine's since their days in Minsk and was a fellow student at the school in Vilna, which, however, he soon left, departing for Paris a short time ahead of Soutine. His friendship with Soutine was never to flag. Through Kikoïne we learn of young Soutine's extremely brilliant career at the school around 1910, a period that marks the beginning of the artist's career, his final break with his early youth, and his determination to submit to his destiny as an artist.

Soutine remained at the school for almost two years. Despite his tender age, his work reveals all the features that were to characterize his art. Impulsive, self-demanding, tortured by his excesses, deliberately destroying anything with which he was dissatisfied, working from nature with the inspiration of instinct, he also affirms his acceptance of the extreme poverty that had tormented him from birth, but that now was relieved by moments of enthusiasm and served as a backdrop for astounding prospects. Soutine dined at the soup kitchen, but went to theatres, rubbed elbows with derelicts as well as brilliant actresses, blended the spectacle of luxury with that of despair, and harmonized within himself the contrasts that were to continue to mark his life and give his work such intensity.

This dark-complexioned, hapless young man with the solemn gaze and the air of an adolescent in a state of self-abandonment received assistance from a charitable organization, and especially from the energetic sympathy of Dr. Reflkess's daughter, who not only introduced him to the works of the great writers but even on one occasion organized a gala in his benefit, the profit from which — fifty rubles — enabled him to travel first to Berlin and then to Paris.

All of this reminds us of van Gogh, an inevitable comparison when we think of this childhood immured in a family group but still more closed within itself, within its obsessions, which were unconscious certitudes, within in the melancholy of the rejections that led to spiritual solitude. Equally evocative of van Gogh are the escape to the city in order to learn the profession that was to be his bondage, his joy, and his unhappiness; the romantic disappointments; the secret love for a young lady; the depressing discovery of the impossibility of an understanding; and the sojourn of several months in a nearby place (London in the case of van Gogh, Vilna in that of Soutine) before the departure for Paris, the magical magnetic pole where the new art styles, Postimpressionism in the case of van Gogh, Fauvism for Soutine, had been developing for some time.

The comparison is also made inevitable by the two artists' common attitude of independence, which was to discover in the new trends an example of daring and freedom but not a model of a technique to be imitated. We find the same combination of humility with self-respect, and finally, and despite instinctive attractions that might have been favorable, always

Photograph of Soutine

18

Photograph of Soutine

the same unconsummated search for communion with others, the same difficulty in communicating feelings — in both cases timidity and pride — that led to a deepening search within the self and to an examination of the great masters of the past.

Equally inevitable is a comparison between the works of the intermediate stage just prior to the flowering into incandescense: between van Gogh's harsh Dutch interiors and the dramatic harshness and painful inspirations of Soutine's Vilna period that, according to his friend Kikoïne, already bore witness to his secret agonies. Among the works dating from this period are burial scenes for which Soutine made his friend pose, stretched out on the ground, surrounded by lighted candles and covered with a white sheet.

Later he would not require this type of complicated setting for the revelation of his interior drama. For the moment it was a step forward over the void of his recent past, a method of escaping from banality and giving material form to his torments, which basically were for him a necessary intensification. He was not yet fully aware of it, but his hell was within him, rather than in the decor he was attempting to devise for himself. In his intimate scenes he attempts to communicate with and nourish his tormented expectations, and in particular he demonstrates his predilection for exaggeration.

In this gray world of his existence in Vilna, Paris must have been to a great extent the mirror of his desires. Paris was above all the place where in recent years something new had been happening, something that was revolutionizing customs and giving corporeal reality to ideas of freedom. The artists seem to have been seized with the delirium of creation, and all of them were dreaming of participating in this feast.

PORTRAIT OF THE PAINTER EMILE LEJEUNE, 1921, Oil, 21¼" x18¾". Walter - Guillaume Collection, Paris

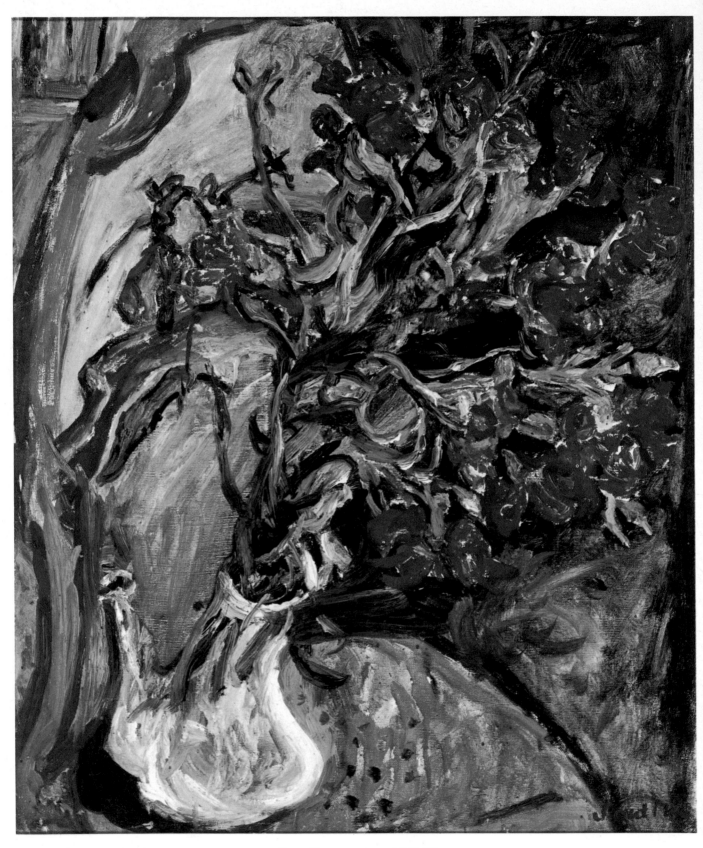

RED CARNATIONS, 1921-22
Oil, 22" x 18³/₈". Coll. Mr. and Mrs. S. J. Levin

GLADIOLAS, 1921-22
Oil, 32½" x 23¾" . Coll. Mr. and Mrs. Ralph Colin, New York

23

SOUTHERN FRENCH LANDSCAPE (VENCE), 1921 Oil, 25½" x 21¼". Musée Calvet, Avignon

24

PARIS, CROSSROADS OF THE WORLD

When Soutine arrived in Paris on July 11, 1911, the art world was seething with excitement. The great movements of artistic renewal had burst upon the scene several years earlier, and artists from every country in the world were beginning to transform the Left Bank into a vast international fair.

Fauvism, since the relatively recent outburst at the Salon d'Automne of 1905, was continuing to provoke daring new ventures among its new adherents, and to surprise a public that had not yet become blasé. Cubism, born of the scandal created by Picasso's already legendary work of 1907, *Les Demoiselles d'Avignon,* was continuing to develop and was constantly enriching its vocabulary of distortions. In 1909 the young Italian artists grouped around Marinetti had chosen Paris at the place from which to launch the Futurist Manifesto, which was a challenge to the past and a call for immediate rebellions in favor of a different future. Young painters arriving from central Europe and Russia were rubbing shoulders with Spaniards, Italians, and Americans, all of them equally impecunious and enthusiastic, all dreaming of entering an enchanted world without a predetermined hierarchy in which everything would be possible for everyone.

For several years this flowering of new ideas and afflux of young artists had been coalescing with another social phenomenon that was rather abruptly modifying relationships between artists and the public, or rather a certain public known as « society » « *les gens du monde* » who dictated the the rules of taste indeed, tyrannies of snobbery.

Until the closing years of the nineteenth century this social class, secure in its supremacy, had viewed the new art forms with contempt. It was now beginning to suspect that in clamorously scorning the Impressionists it had let slip a splendid moral opportunity to appear in the guise of guide of public opinion, and a financial opportunity to build up splendid collections.

To be sure, the established art was still enjoying great prestige, and the opening of the Salon continued to be the artistic event of the year. Suddenly, the revelation of Serge Diaghilev's Ballets Russes in 1908, with their considerable and somewhat scandalous success, introduced a breath of fresh air into this dull routine. The snobs were discovering the pleasure of dabbling in the audacities of the new and the picturesque quality of provocation, thereby immediately revealing their susceptibility to extreme positions. Even feminine fashion, hitherto so circumspect, now became deliberately eccentric, and no longer retreated in the face of possible disapproval. This explains the great excitement with which Fauvism, and above all Cubism, were quickly greeted. Even if collectors were still few in number and paintings were selling for low prices, the interest taken in avant-garde activities was not limited to the narrow circle of young artists, and awakened favorable echoes, or at least an active curiosity, in the elegant salons. This new expansion of intellectual horizons was helpful to all artists; it contributed unexpected ideas, and a foreign origin was no longer a handicap but an asset. This fact explains and justifies in large part the attraction exerted by Paris on the world.

Soutine immediately became part of this cosmopolitan group. Through his friend Kikoïne he found lodging in La Ruche, a bizarre caravansary consisting of a picturesque ramshackle building rescued by the sculptor Dubois from the demolition of the pavilions of the International Exposition of 1900, reerected for better or worse near the Vaugirard slaughterhouses in the Passage de Dantzig, and now welcoming the poverty-stricken bohemians of politics and the arts, to whom it offered a cramped and precarious shelter for the reasonable rent of one hundred francs a year.

Here Soutine met artists who had arrived in Paris a short time before him, who shared his enthusiasm and were brothers in fervor and in their total poverty. In addition to Kikoïne, who had preceded him here, they included Kremegne (another compatriot and friend), Chagall, Fernand Léger, Robert Delaunay, and Blaise Cendrars, as well as Laurens, Zadkine, and Archipenko, all of whom lived in La Ruche for varying periods of time but sought a less precarious shelter at the first opportunity. (Soutine himself left it as soon as possible.)

It is easy to visualize the dizzy atmosphere that must have reigned in these circles in which everyone was young, totally lacking in material resources, and not yet completely involved in his destiny, at a time when the material meanness connected with early successes had not yet made human relations more difficult and less altruistic. Everyone in this world was just beginning his career and, seemingly at least, each had the same opportunities. Soutine was the junior member of this motley group — Léger had been born in 1881, Chagall in 1887, Zadkine in 1890. Several of the artists already had a past, and sometimes the beginning of a reputation in the admittedly limited circles of this avant-garde that was beginning to spread and be noticed.

Soutine was still too close to his years of apprenticeship to venture into the hazardous world of individual creativity. Realizing his lack of experience, and feeling that he had something to learn from the teaching of older artists, he registered at that home of the academic and «established» art, the Ecole des Beaux-Arts and also joined the studio of the painter Cormon, who could not be considererd a defender of innovative viewpoints. It is not clear what Soutine's impulsive temperament could have gained from this confrontation with such extremely conventional instruction, nor how his need to exteriorize the depths of the human soul could have been adapted to his teacher's scrupulous historical reconstructions, unless we believe that the effect of this contrast was the heightening of Soutine's predilection for the most spontaneous expression and the confirmation of his own temperament.

His discoveries at the Louvre, the goal of his first excursions in Paris, were to be more in harmony with his tastes. Waldemar George gives us a lively portrait of Soutine in his description of his first meeting there with the painter.

« One morning, under the diffuse light of the Ile-de-France, I saw a young foreigner with a low forehead and a shifting gaze standing in front of *The Burial at Ornans*. Seemingly frightened, he kept very close to the wall, and moved away as soon as anyone came near him. He was looking at the works of the early masters much as a believer looks at sacred pictures. My curiosity led me to follow him through the rooms of the museum. Several hours later, apparently sated, he moved toward the exit of the Louvre. He stópped before Ingre's *The Spring*, went down the stairs, and retrieved from the coatroom a small suitcase which undoubtedly contained his belongings. Two or three years later I became acquainted with him. It was Chaim Soutine. »

In another text Waldemar George gives us an even more precise portrait. « He walked slowly, with a slumped posture, staying close to the walls as if fleeing a ghost or a phantom. His face occasionally lighted up with a childlike smile, and his eyes laughed. He had the hands of a virtuoso, with long, slender fingers. His door was closed to unwelcome visitors, but he could be polite. His insolence and his fits of rage concealed a withdrawn, timid nature. » Everyone who knew him stressed the elegance of Soutine's hands and the timidity that caused him to be considered hostile.

This meeting with the work of Courbet, and the long study (repeated on several other occasions) of *The Burial at Ornans,* are important events, inasmuch as they supply one of the keys to Soutine's art.

If we endeavor to see the facts as they are, we are forced to recognize that Courbet's large composition with its parade of mourners, whose brightly colored, bloated faces are painted in heavy impasto and whose features are accentuated to the point of caricature, was at very least an unusual sight on the traditional walls of a museum, and an invitation to nonconformism. It is understandable that the unsociable Soutine must have been overwhelmed by this discovery, by the freedom of language that had succeeded in conquering the vainglory of this queen of museums.

Courbet's realism surpasses visible reality, and Soutine more than any other artist was capable of understanding the profound freedom and even aggressiveness of this language. He was able to see in it not only an example of freedom of technique equivalent to the freedom he felt developing within himself, but also a social attitude, a statement by a human being about human beings that corresponded to his own demands, his own intransigence, and the goal toward which he was moving, even if unconsciously. It it possible to believe that Courbet aided in his growth of self-awareness, at a period when his ideas were still somewhat chaotic because of the abundance of ideas and temptations that assail every young man. Courbet was the incarnation of everything Soutine was seeking: independence of thought, rigor in rebellion, the simple grandeur of the dramatic sense, and inspired freedom of technique.

Another and equally essential miracle at the Louvre was Soutine's encounter with Rembrandt. The bond between these two artists would be immediately apparent even if Soutine had not later painted similar subjects in his *Carcass of Beef* and *Woman Bathing.* While Courbet provided him with an example of the liberated, creative violence of a personal language and a reality affirmed to the point of seeming exaggerated, Rembrant's contribution, in contrast, was the magic of mysterious transfigurations, thick buildups of paint that become enchanting illuminations, and brushstrokes that when individually considered seem random but acquire intensely alive and precise shapes when viewed as a whole. In Rembrandt's works

Soutine was able to discover the constantly renewed, shifting play of colors in relation to one another, and, beyond this technical virtuosity, the possibility of achieving the summit of human expression: the poignant exploration and externalization of the inner life.

We can imagine him anxiously interrogating the faces re-created by Rembrandt, like palpitating flesh born of shadow and light: we can visualize him understanding the moving beauty of the flesh born of the painter's will. Later, in the various versions of the *Woman Bathing*, he was to repeat the theme depicted by Rembrandt in the painting in the National Gallery. Rembrandt more than any other artist was able to arouse Soutine's awareness and awaken him to his own nature by convincing him of the essential role of the imagination.

In this connection, Waldemar George notes that «He was a tireless visitor to the Louvre, and paid four visits to The Hague, where he spent endless hours before *The Jewish Bride*.» Chana Orloff, who knew Soutine very well, writes, «I still see him approaching Rembrandt's canvases with a kind of respectful fear. He stood for a long time, went into a trance, and pranced about shouting, "It's so beautiful it maddens me!" The alarmed guard followed us. . .»

We are reminded increasingly of van Gogh when we contemplate this passion for painting, this predilection for seizing upon the image of the external world in order to heighten and dramatize it by the use of vigorously ground pigments. In comparison, however, with the increased vehemence brought to this image by Soutine, van Gogh's intensity takes on an appearance of order. His broad strokes are arranged, notwithstanding their vigor and spontaneity, in equal, fairly even parallel rows. Soutine's painting, on the other hand, is a ruthless impulse, a disordered gush, a chaotic and random buildup of a magma from which, by some unknown miracle, there emerge the details of a face, the body of a bird, or a bouquet of flowers.

Van Gogh's classicism becomes very apparent in the presence of Soutine's phantasmagoria, although we are aware of the existence in both artists of a barely contained passion. Soutine's pathos is exteriorized in a more theatrical efflorescence, and it enables him to stress the two attitudes possible for a human being in the grip of the forces of an inflexible passion, one controlled and disciplined, the other abandoned to itself like a rushing torrent or like molten lava gushing from a volcano.

His arrival in France coincided with the period most favorable for unlimited expansion, when everything was seemingly becoming possible because everything was being challenged; the best artists were rejecting the limitations of reality, poets were discovering areas of agreement with the most independent painters, and the limits to creativity seemed to have no bounds. From this understanding between literature and the arts was born a constant exchange of ideas, and we are not certain whether it was the daring experiments of the painters that called forth original observations by the writers, or whether the development by the latter of unexpected forms encouraged the artists to escape from the traditional forms of representation.

The progress made by science and mechanics certainly was not irrelevant to this tremendous proliferation of ideas, which thanks to their discoveries bordered on what is today

HOUSE WITH TREE (SOUTHERN FRENCH LANDSCAPE), 1922-23 Oil, private collection

LITTLE GIRL IN THE MEADOW, 1920
Oil, 18" x 21¼"
Perls Galleries, New York

THE OLD MILL, ca. 1922
Oil, 26¹/₈" x 32³/₈"
Museum of Modern Art, New York

THE MADWOMAN
1921-22
Oil
Private Collection

THE PASTRY COOK WITH RED HANDKERCHIEF, 1922-23
Oil, 28¾" x 21½". Walter - Guillaume Collection, Paris

SIDE OF BEEF, 1922-23
Oil, 27½" x 20½". Coll. Mr. and Mrs. Ralph Colin, New York

34

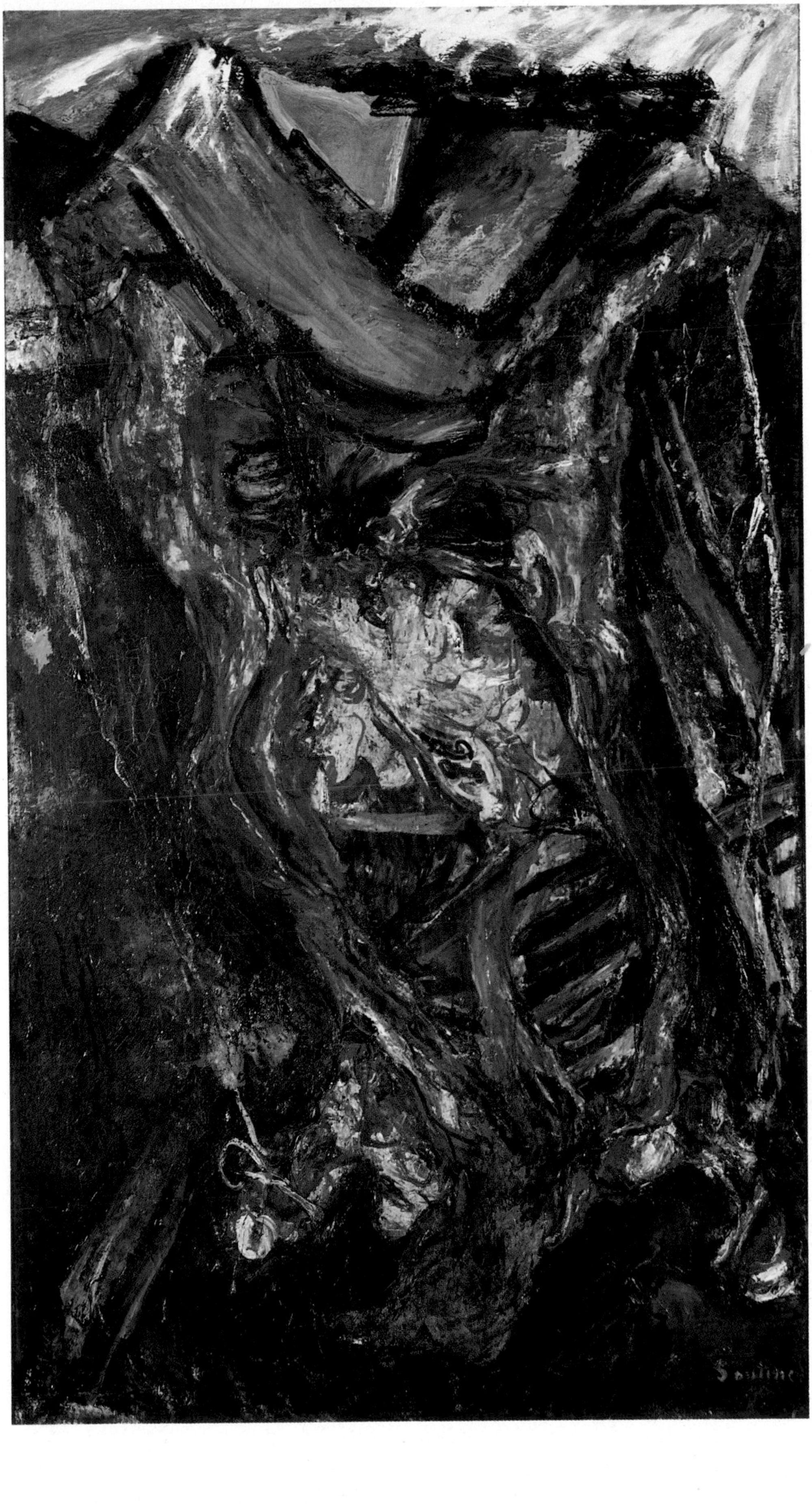

CARCASS OF BEEF, 1925
Oil, 84¼" x 47½"
Musée de Grenoble

RAYFISH, ca. 1924
Oil, 32" x 39½"
Perls Galleries, New York

STILL LIFE WITH RAYFISH
Oil, 32" x 25⅝" L
Cleveland Museum of Art

36

37

DEAD FOWL, ca. 1924
Oil, 43½" x 32" . Museum of Modern Art, New York

Rabbit with Iron Pot, 1925
Oil, 32½" x 15"
Walter - Guillaume Collection, Paris

FISH AND TOMATOES, 1926-27
Oil, 24¼" x 32"
Coll. Mr. and Mrs. Jack I. Poses, New York

known as science fiction. From their inception aviation and the cinema, the phonograph and the automobile, aroused the artists' interest and profoundly altered the climate of intellectual circles.

The social environment was also being transformed in an unexpected manner. Hitherto most artists had been members of the financially comfortable middle class, where their position was to a certain extent that of difficult children who nevertheless shared class conventions that influenced their choice of both thermes and techniques. Even their rebellions, which in certain cases extended to political anarchy, corresponded to attitudes and systems of reasoning characteristic of intellectuals. Their art, whether Impressionist, Neo-Impressionist, or Nabi, was an art of refined and cultured individuals who participated in the life-style of an untroubled, economically comfortable social class in which change occurred through evolution, not revolution.

This psychological and social climate began to change in the twentieth century. Fauvism, Cubism, Expressionism, and Futurism made their appearance with a ruthlessness that was categorically opposed to everything that had preceded them. Some of the artists who created these movements came of modest or even proletarian stock; they had no love for nuances and halfway measures, and violently proclaimed their desire to change the world.

Even those who by tradition or family origin were able to retain their link with the past outdid each other in exaggeration in order not to be left behind, to the point that one of the most provocative movements — Futurism, which in proclaiming the Futurist movement in France went to the extreme of urging the destruction of museums — originated in that most traditional of countries, Italy. The new artists blew into the warm softness of tradition not a breath of fresh air but the beginnings of a tornado, and it was this combative vigor that attracted foreigners still trapped by their national inhibitions.

In view of the powerful attraction exerted by the ideas current at this time and rendered extremely contagious by their dynamism and novelty, it is astonishing that Soutine, although in direct and constant contact with the ideas and works, and despite his friendship with several of their creators, never participated in one of these movements, was never even tempted to experiment with their ideas, and maintained complete independence. It is impossible to establish the slightest relationship between his art and that produced by the great currents that came into existence before the First World War.

To begin with, the persistence of a certain order and discipline is always evident in artistic innovations in France, even at their most daring and eccentric. Even in Fauvist and Cubist works, creativity always went hand in hand with a constant scrutiny of the methods used. This is true of both Matisse and Picasso, and even more so of Fernand Léger and Derain, Braque, and Vlaminck, the current leaders of movements. Here we are obviously at the opposite pole of what was to be Soutine's art, with its dramatic spontaneity and frenzied improvisation.

THE BIRTH OF JEWISH PAINTING

Perhaps another element should be introduced at this point, and with it a source of inspiration that instead of placing Soutine's work within the context of French art would relate it instead to the Expressionist current then being developed in Germany. The matter looks completely different when viewed from this angle, and we are led to think that a parenthesis should be opened in the story of European art for an attempted definition of a Jewish art style created to a large extent by the artists of central Europe, fortuitously congregated at this time in a flight from the menace of ill-treatment and racial hatred that promised to grow worse.

This idea of a Jewish style of painting is one of the most widely discussed problems of contemporary art. Many critics refuse to accept such a designation, claiming that it does not correspond to a well-defined set of specifics. The fact is that prior to the twentieth century no demarcation of the characteristics of what could be a Jewish art within the living art of Europe can be formulated, probably in part because respect for religious dogma eliminated any idea of representation and hence the possibility of a role in European art, which has a strong predilection for representation and realism of images. Moreover, it would be incorrect and inaccurate to place the handful of nineteenth-century European Jewish painters in this special category, because at that time they were not distinguished in any way from the other, Christian artists of the same period.

Beginning in the twentieth century, and particularly after Soutine, the situation changes completely, probably as the result of particular social conditions rather than for sectarian reasons. Several artists from central Europe and Russia have introduced a very special note into the art of our age, a feeling for the pathos of daily life, a latent despair, or even simply a melancholy and a resignation, forms of Eastern fatalism expressed in the choice of themes and style.

Their style shuns the previously accepted rules, and finds its strength in the great freedom it discovers in the grinding of the colored impasto, crushed onto the canvas in heavy, broad brushstrokes seemingly controlled by an inspiration that is always in a state of overstimulation instead of being held in check by the rules of an aesthetic system. This state of affairs seems to be the consequence of a state of mind resulting from political circumstances and the climate of permanent anxiety in which the Jews of certain areas live. When upon their arrival in the Western countries they suddenly discover a relaxed atmosphere, they give free rein to the hitherto suppressed nostalgia to which they had become accustomed. Their right to create something drives them like a torrent liberated after centuries of restraints.

In a note he sent me for a text I was preparing on Soutine, his friend Kikoïne

Photograph of Soutine by Roger Viollet

makes a very precise reference to this phenomenon of the birth of Jewish painting at the beginning of the twentieth century, and gives the reasons for its particularism and the artists' consciousness of it. He writes, « Soutine and we other Jewish painters exiled in a foreign country were constantly preoccupied with another drama, that of the absence of a pictorial tradition, which the artistic culture of the adopted country did not succeed in counterbalancing. »

Thus the seeming chaos of Soutine's art is not decadence or degeneracy; on the contrary, it is a vital force that explodes forms without any need to refer to traditions of any kind. Even though we are discussing a Jewish art, we should not look too hard for a connection with some Talmudic prohibition abruptly transgressed and swept away by an overflowing of freedom, but rather (and especially in the case of Soutine) a cry harshly contained within itself, a cry that tends to become a form still in gestation in that phase of creation in which the best and the worst coexist in potentiality. This is the basis for our opinion that a Jewish art was born with Soutine.

When the war broke out in August 1914, Soutine obtained a residence permit, and lived for a time in Franceville in the suburbs of Paris, where his friends the Kikoïnes had rented a one-family house after their departure from La Ruche. Shortly thereafter, in a desire to serve France, he enlisted with the workers, but poor health cut this effort short, and he returned to Paris, where after his departure from La Ruche he occupied a studio in the Cité Falguière.

He soon became friendly with, among the other artists living there, two Russian sculptors who were to play an important role in the Paris School, the first elements of which were beginning to coalesce at this time. One was Jacques Lipchitz, who would be a major factor in the creation of Cubist sculpture; the other was Mietschaninoff, one of the most active members of this young avant-garde.

In 1915 Lipchitz introduced Soutine to a young Italian painter named Amedeo Modigliani. Despite major differences, even diametrical opposition of temperament and artistic style, the two men became friends. Their daily association was marked by sharp clashes, and we are justified in believing that Soutine did not always feel at ease with Modigliani. In the words of Chana Orloff:

«He hated to mention his friendship with Modigliani, and gave vent to his rancor along with his memories, going so far as to say that Modigliani's painting was not painting. He never forgave Modigliani for involving him in drinking. I am not sure that their relationship deserved the name of friendship. Who was not Modigliani's friend at a bar, elbow to elbow before a glass of red wine? Soutine and Modigliani were two companion hermits. . . . Alcohol did Soutine a great deal of harm. »

It is also possible that despite its initial spontaneity, their friendship, fostered by the extreme poverty they shared, was also damaged by this same poverty. In particular, however, it may have been blunted by the inflexibility of both men and by the clash of their fundamental differences: Modigliani's outgoing nature versus Soutine's apprehensive withdrawal, the violence of Soutine's art as contrasted with the calm, controlled, systematic compositions

CHOIRBOY WITH SURPLICE, ca. 1928, Oil, 25" x 19¾". Walter - Guillaume Collection, Paris

45

46

BUST OF A WOMAN AGAINST A BLUE GROUND, 1927-28
Oil, 17½" x 20"
Musée d'Art Moderne de la Ville de Paris

WOMAN IN BLUE DRESS, ca. 1924-25
Oil, 31⁷/₈" x 23⁵/₈"
Musée d'Art Moderne de la Ville de Paris

47

VALET IN BURGUNDY JACKET, 1927-28
48 Oil, 25½" x 19¼". Coll. Mr. and Mrs. Nathan Cummings, New York

THE VALET, 1928
Oil, 36¼" x 25⅝". National Gallery of Art, Washington, D.C.

49

THE HEAD VALET, 1928
Oil, 34" x 26"
Walter - Guillaume Collection, Paris

PORTRAIT OF MADELEINE CASTAING, 1928
Oil, 39³/₈ x 28⁷/₈"
Metropolitan Museum of Art, New York

SLEEPING WOMAN, 1928, Oil, 17¹/₁₆" x 13¾". Coll. Mr. and Mrs. John A. Beck, Houston, Texas

SOUTINE

Soutine

By Raymond Cogniat

CROWN PUBLISHERS, INC. - NEW YORK

Title Page Illustration: PORTRAIT OF SOUTINE
by Terechkovitch
1933, oil, 27¾" x 19¾"
Musée de Menton

Translated by:
EILEEN B. HENNESSY

Photographs: E. Dulière, Brussels - Giraudon, Paris - Otto Nelson,
New York - Photopress, Grenoble - Roger Viollet, Paris

ISBN 0517 511363
LIBRARY OF CONGRESS CATALOG CARD NUMBER: 73-84255
ALL REPRODUCTION RIGHTS TO THE PHOTOGRAPHS BY S.P.A.D.E.M. PARIS
PRINTED IN ITALY BY VALLARDI INDUSTRIE GRAFICHE - MILAN - © 1973 BY
PALLAS SCRIPT AGENCY S. A. NAEFELS, SUISSE
ALL RIGHTS IN THE U.S.A. ARE RESERVED BY CROWN PUBLISHERS, INC., NEW YORK, N.Y.

SCENE NEAR CHARTRES, undated
Oil, 18½" x 21½"
Coll. Mr. and Mrs. Nathan Cummings, New York

ANTIBOURGEOIS ART

Each person is at once an exceptional being and a representative of his age, a unique individual and a synthesis of what others are. Each individual can stand as a symbol. Soutine and his fate epitomize this summary definition. For this reason a survey of the principal physical and spiritual traits that define Soutine's personality is not without value.

It is true that analysis of an age, like that of a human being, tends to metamorphose it into a unique moment, an unfolding of events that are at variance with the logic that ordered the other moments of history. The nineteenth century, however little we may linger over it, represents for us a major change in the analysis of our society and even our civilization, both in a spiritual sense, by the nature of the individual's relations with the social structures around him, and in a material one, through upheavals in science and the practical changes that thereby transform daily existence.

The adaptation of the human being even to improved ways of living and thinking inevitably gives rise to difficulties, and it is not always possible to make a clear distinction between good and bad. For example, freedoms collectively achieved have as their corollary individual doubts and hesitations in making personal choices, and they engender difficult adaptations to a different order. In the nineteenth century misunderstandings between artist and public arose from that freedom which creates unforeseeable conflicts between the rights of the creator over his creation and those of consumer over the pleasure he expects to find in the ownership or contemplation of a work of art. Liberty is a burdensome privilege for those who appeal to it as their authority, and neither artist nor public can be held responible for the dissension that sets them at odds.

This lack of harmony nevertheless gave birth to the « *artiste maudit,* » the artist laboring under a curse, a social category, rare in earlier centuries, which inevitably selects its victims from among individuals worthy of admiration. Soutine is the perfect prototype of this irremediable lack of adaptation, which places the individual and his instinct in opposition to every aspect of his surroundings. But this opposition, although fundamental, does not mean that the artist is alien to his age; on the contrary, his isolation is extremely significant and inevitable.

Within the system of the affirmation of material demands and ambitions born in the nineteenth century it was believed that spiritual values could be regarded merely as incidental problems. The indifference with which they were treated at this time hindered their normal incorporation into society and its fundamental structures, but it could not eliminate them. These spiritual values therefore developed in a climate of pseudoindependence and above all of solitude, which welcomed them with indifference and left them their freedom, thereby aiding their development but at the same time exacerbating their need to escape from that solitude and emerge into the open. The social phenomenon of the « accursed, » seemingly asocial artist is thus the living symbol of an age that did not fully comprehend the complexity of his needs and resources.

Thus the isolated individual constitutes a category and a class whose assimilation is rendered even less successful and more embittered by the fact that it corresponds not to a deliberate choice by the individual concerned but to an ineluctable predestination that affects every milieu, rich or poor, learned or ignorant, without distinction. At the end of the nineteenth century this development became an increasingly widespread historical fact, and began to assume active forms, leading to the development of the anarchist movements and

6

their direct intervention in public life. Soutine, who was born in 1893, thus came into the world at a time when this tension was becoming general throughout Europe and was assuming still more intense forms in those countries whose political regimes were, thanks to their resistance to change or their indecisiveness, provoking increasingly vigorous reactions. His life and his work must be considered from this viewpoint of inevitable protest.

However, the violence that was to characterize his art and his behavior must not be viewed merely as a combination of a conflict of social apposition with internal inconsistencies. Such an explanation would be incomplete, because there are both a permanency and a constancy in this supposed disorder that become a form of unity. This has enabled certain critics to speak of classicism, and thus to discover and emphasize a certain order in this continuity. Soutine did not have to adopt attitudes in accordance with circumstances; more simply, he should be seen as a passionate individual, all of whose activities bore the stamp of a need for the absolute, a person whom nothing could dissuade from following the imperatives of his vocation. Moreover, the evidence of this vocation impressed itself upon him at a very early age, and he tenaciously imposed it upon his family.

THE FORMATIVE YEARS

He was born, as we have said, in 1893, into a very humble family (his father was a tailor) in Smilovitchi, a small village near Minsk, in Belorussia. Let us not unduly dramatize his unhappy life from its beginning, in order to discover certain harbingers of the future, nor accuse others of unpardonable blindness. No humble village tailor has ever thought to provide for his son's future by making an artist of him. A tradition-bound family and a small, quiet town do not inevitably crush a normal person, but they do constrain the exceptional individual. Mutual misunderstandings, exacerbated by the harsh limitations of extreme poverty, produce a child martyr, and anecdotes later recalled become a justification for future rebellions. It is too often thought that unhappy people are the victims of systematically hostile surroundings. The truth is that it is generally the individuals themselves who bear their fate within them, regardless of what they do; the outside world plays only a secondary role.

Chaim Soutine, a timid, passionate child, was painfully sensitive to the blows of life, more because of his nature than because of the ill will of those around him. He led the harsh life common to the children of the poor, and the fact that (according to one story) he stole a cooking pot in order to purchase color pencils is not necessarily proof of an irresistible vocation, any more than his subsequent punishment is a proof of domestic tyranny. It is likely, of course, that Chaim's extreme sensitivity caused him to be delicate and out of harmony with his surroundings. Pierre Courthion tells us that the boy fainted at the sight of the fowls ritually flayed for holiday feasts, a detail to be kept in mind.

All of this, however, is not enough to make him a victim, and while his father would have preferred to see him choose an occupation other than that of painter (a rabbi, according to some stories; a shoemaker, according to others), he did not categorically oppose the child's obvious aptitude for drawing. At the age of ten Chaim went to work for a tailor (the brother-in-law of his eldest sister), but he very soon in 1907 abandoned this apprenticeship in favor of a photographer's studio in Minsk, where he did enlarging and retouching. This activity was far more in harmony with his taste and talents, to the point that a doctor who was interested in him advised that he be given drawing lesson. A certain Kreuger thus became his teacher in Minsk.

From this moment Soutine's future seems to have been determined, and confirmed also by his friendship at this time with another young man, Kikoïne, whose destiny from then on unfolded in a direction parallel to that of Soutine. There is also the oft-told story of the beating given young Chaim by several children because he had done the portrait of an elderly village Jew. Other biographers state that he was « beaten by the butcher because he had painted the rabbi. » The butcher was the rabbi's son, and was angered because this portrait violated the prohibition against depicting the human figure and was thus a kind of sacrilege. The result

8

of Modigliani. The contrasting qualities that had at first attracted them may later have set them at odds.

The clashes were certainly exacerbated, if not actually caused, by alcoholism. Soutine was obliged on occasion to sober up, forced into greater moderation by stomach problems. But as soon as these crises were over, he again allowed himself to be led astray by his confederate, mesmerized by the latter's ebullience and at the same time irritated by his own submission to it. The chaos of this impromptu existence was accompanied by extreme poverty, and here again the detached and alluring Modigliani with his lordly air stood in contrast to Soutine with his timid, hunted demeanor.

This total dissimilarity extended to their art. The basis of Modigliani's art was clean, precise draftsmanship, delimiting paint laid on in broad areas, in scarcely modeled planes, and utilizing a limited palette, producing calm, melancholy compositions that were almost exclusively full-length portraits with contours that verged on the geometrical, with transparent eyes lost in dream. Soutine's was an art of ruthless impulses, of colors superimposed seemingly at random, jostling and overlapping each other, of deformed human figures, of surfaces in a state of constant movement, providing no repose and no area of relaxation for mind and eye. In any event, this turbulent friendship played an essential role in Soutine's life, and provided daily nourishment for his need to live in an atmosphere of intense emotion.

Naturally his painting was not salable. Cheron, an art dealer in the Rue La Boétie who had accepted Soutine on Modigliani's recommendation, readily encouraged these artists to paint by supplying them with bottles of red wine and paying between forty and sixty francs for one of their paintings. His support was small and erratic, however. A tiny group of patrons completed this limited clientele; they included. Dr. Devraigne, two commissioners named Descaves and Zameron, and (slightly later) Messrs. Dutilleul and Hugues Simon.

Modigliani also introduced Soutine to Zborowski, a Polish poet turned art dealer for the occasion, who became enthusiastic about this painter and contributed the very modest sum of five francs a day for his support. Thanks to him a major portion of Soutine's output was saved from destruction. Soutine sometimes went for long periods without working, permitting his mind to wander or to develop, in a state of dreary idleness, the work of art that would later gush forth with seeming spontaneity and irresistible drive. Then, when he did paint, he did so quickly, with the passion of a man inspired. Frequently, however, dissatisfied with what he was doing as contrasted with what he wanted to express, he destroyed the works he no longer liked. Zborowski found ways of keeping the carnage within bounds, but this situation worsened as time went on, a fact that explains why few canvases from his early years are still extant.

The catalogue of Soutine's paintings just published by Pierre Courthion lists barely fifteen canvases that could have been painted before 1915. They are a very early manifestation of his predilection for impastos and bright colors that nevertheless form refined relationships. They also show a certain severity, and even sometimes, particularly in a few landscapes, a certain stiffness that is ill suited for the translation of the movements of this soul in its state of constant excitement, revealing of an inhibition that has not been fully overcome. A

53

view of the studio in the Cité Falguière and a self-portrait are indicative of this difficulty in adapting technical discipline to natural drives. Soutine was very quickly to discover a style of his own, a style of constant movement, consisting of superimposed surges and jostling, overlapping, interlacing whirlpools of paint that invade the entire surface of the canvas.

To be convinced of this we need only compare two pictures from this period: *Woman Lying on a Couch* (1915 - 1916) and *Woman Lying on the Grass* (1916 - 1917), in which we see an accentuation of the violence and a softening of that stiffness we mentioned in connection with the 1916 portrait. There is a certain languid grace in the earlier painting, unusual in Soutine's work, and a sureness of hand thanks to which the brush and the paint draw and directly model the forms, giving the pictorial material its full sensuousness. This power becomes more brutal in the later painting, which is hard and rugged and reminiscent of a similar theme treated by Courbet, who was at this time the object of Soutine's vigorous admiration.

Other extant paintings of this period (1915 - 1916) help to complete the picture of a tormented mind, thoroughly impregnated by the misery of daily life, and to pave the way for his final orientation toward a more turbulent style. The landscapes take on a sense of catastrophe, but the portraits are still relatively calm, with a few disquieting distortions. The still lifes in particular strive to remain within a bare, linear sobriety that emphasizes the pathos in their extreme simplicity. One painting, entitled *Still Life with Pipe*, has the austere, at once dark and shining atmosphere sometimes seen in the works of Vlaminck. The fish compositions must also be studied, especially the painting of three herrings lying on an oval plate and threatened by two forks; its despairing, aggressive realism is reminiscent of the dramatic feeling that emanates from the worn shoes painted by van Gogh as an incarnation of implacable misery.

For van Gogh the south of France was an experience so overwhelming that it caused his painting to become totally committed to its definitive path and inspired in him an unrestrained lyricism. It seems clear that Soutine experienced a similar reaction. In 1918, still with Zborowski's assistance, and in the company of Modigliani, he settled in Vence, and immediately came under the spell of this region. But whereas van Gogh abandoned himself to its spell without foregoing a certain discipline that sustained him, even in extreme states, within a tradition of order that can be called classical, Soutine permitted his drives complete liberty and his vision an increase in violence and intensity. Compared with what he was to produce henceforth, his earlier works seem almost calm, and the harmony of nature, though intense, revealed to him his own lack of moderation. A strange phenomenon now occurred. Instead of letting hinself being charmed and won over by this abundant natural world, he ruthlessly took possession of it, bent it to his will, exaggerated its vehement vegetable growths, intensified its colors but turned his back on its calm, overlooked the notion of static time so peculiar to Provence. In fact, liberated by it, he imposed his nature and the rhythm of his passion on it. His art now fully attained its apocalyptic character and became a suitable vehicle for the painful revelation of its creator, who continued to live in materially deplorable conditions, wretchedly lodged and fed, in a state of constant tension, increasingly harassed by his stomach troubles.

Portrait of Soutine
by Modigliani

55

Successive periods of residence in Cagnes and Céret confined him to the same atmosphere of fervor and creation. His work of that time expresses passion for life as well as rage in the face of a world whose zest for life is a constant provocation to him, for the Mediterranean coastal area where he was living is all joyous radiance, in contrast to the relatively austere area around Arles familiar to van Gogh. Soutine's production now became more abundant, consisting almost exclusively of landscapes and still lifes, including those extraordinarily twisted gladioli bleeding like open sores. Contrary to what one might believe, Soutine painted from nature, distorting it once he had become throughly acquainted with it. He acquires an intimate awareness of it and forces it to surrender; one can say without great exaggeration that he violates it. One of his models has told of being made to pose for a long time before he actually set to work, which he did once the individual, denuded of all surface appearances that conceal its profound truth, had become an object, once the exhausting wait had become almost a hallucinatory experience for both of them. Once this moment had arrived, Soutine painted the work with feverish haste. Thus his seeming rejection of nature is actually a form of taking possession, of conquest; it signals the primacy of the individual human being over the reality of the external world, henceforth subjugated to his will and his thought to the point of becoming caricatural, even in his landscapes. Here he again differs from his contemporaries, for the Fauves, and especially the Cubists, deny nature or attempt to destroy it, while Soutine embraces, explores, and tyrannizes over it.

The twisting road mounts to the assault on the countryside. The houses, in the grip of frenzy, dance an uninhibited saraband. Soutine's vision becomes a monstrous distorting mirror in which nature at its most serene loses all stability. A world in fury stands revealed in all its delirious splendor.

Perhaps it was because he was totally lacking in worldly possessions and lived as humbly as a farm animal in its stable that Soutine completely broke all restraints and poured out the treasures of his dreams. After Vence, with its immense tree shining like the Burning Bush, and its streets twisted by a cataclysm, Céret is in flames. Everywhere trees and houses twist under the effect of the cyclone. When, rarely, a house seems to be still standing upright, it appears to be miraculously balanced on the edge of a precipice seconds before being swallowed up. When we look at several paintings from this period placed side by side in a book, we are struck by this continuity in chaos, and by the terrible visionary message, which, like a reading of the Apocalypse of St. John, makes us feel that we are experiencing an agonizing obsession with and affirmation of catastrophe couched in the form not of a probable future but of a visible, present reality. This is testimony, not prophecy.

PORTRAIT OF BOY IN BLUE, 1929, Oil, 30" x 23"
Coll. Mr. and Mrs. Ralph Colin, New York . Property of Ralph F. Colin Jr.

TREE AT VENCE, 1929
Oil, 31⁷/₈" x 24¹/₈". Coll. Mrs. Bruce Westcott. Rosemont, N.J.

58

SMALL
OWN SQUARE,
ence, ca. 1930
, 28" x 18¼"
Art Institute,
Chicago

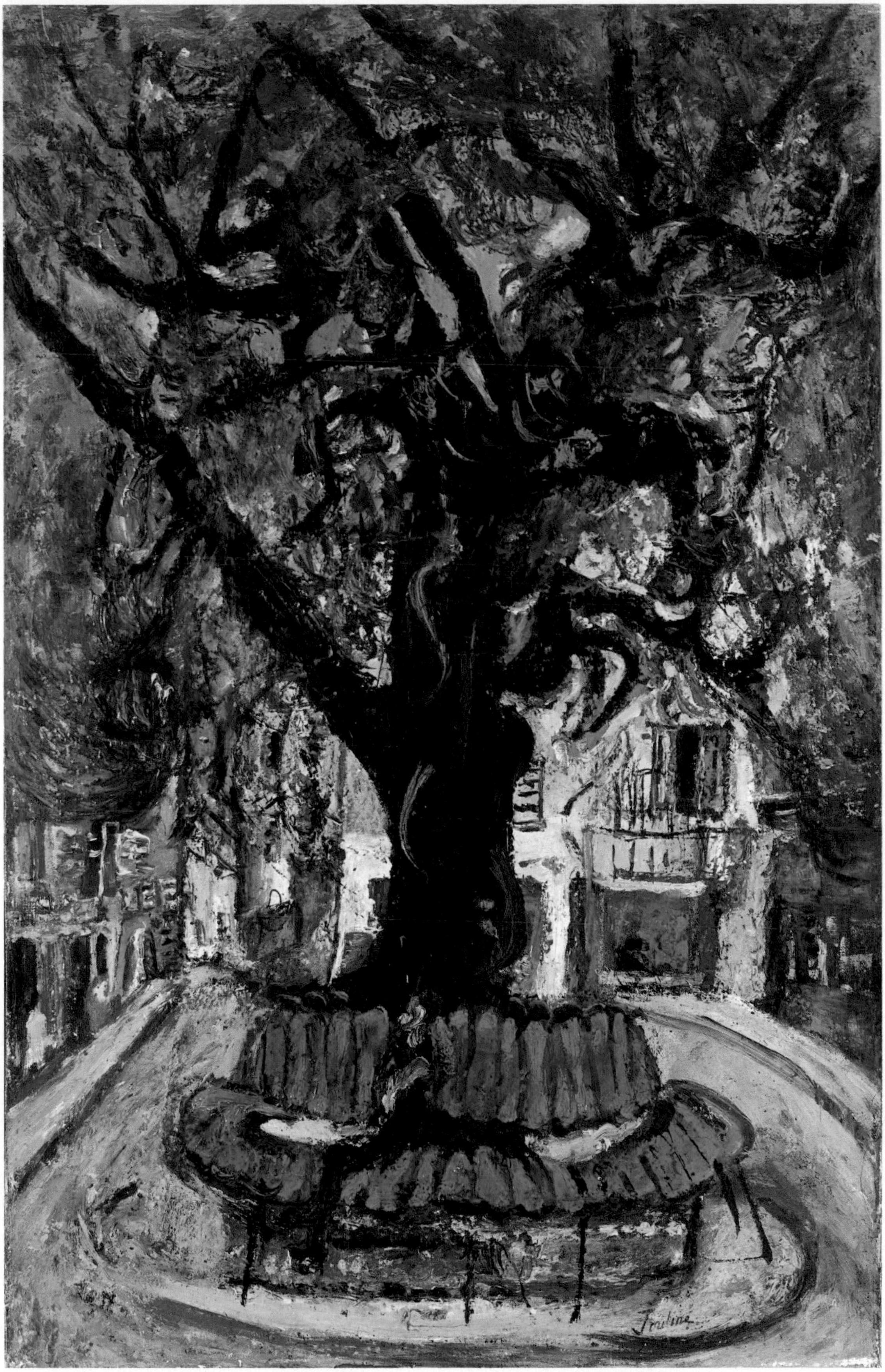

FLIGHT OF STAIRS IN CHARTRES, 1933
Oil, 17" x 10⁵/₈". Coll. Mr. and Mrs. Jack I. Poses, New York

ɪARTRES CATHEDRAL, 1933
Oil, 36" x 19½"
Museum of Modern Art,
New York

THE PAGE BOY AT MAXIM'S, 1933
Oil, 16" x 13¹/₈". Musée National d'Art Moderne, Paris

ɔMAN IN PROFILE, 1937
Oil, 18½" x 11"
Phillips Gallery,
Washington, D.C.

YOUNG GIRL WITH A DOLL, ca. 1932
Oil, 23¾" x 19". Coll. Mr. and Mrs. John A. Beck, Houston, Texas

64

THE CHARM OF UGLINESS

Soutine exposes his errant soul to us in the incessant, luxuriant whirlpool of forms and colors with which he is hallucinated. His frenzy soon begins to spread to his human figures. He attacks this subject with a more muted anxiety, a more secret and profound interrogation. He seems to be overcome by terror before these faces opening to him that he can no longer ignore, faces irremediably marked by their defects. Their stupidity, vulgarity, hypocrisy, and greed, hunted to earth by his implacable observation, are henceforth to haunt his visions, destroying all surface harmonies, obliterating the agreeable features, and super-imposing upon them the furrows of anxieties and involuntary confessions. We may well believe that the cruelty he shows in the observation and depiction of human beings is in large part a translation of disappointed love, a part of his great pity for humanity, for the ordinary mortal assailed by unhappiness and by physical as well as spiritual flaws. We feel more than ever that love and blasphemy spring from the same source and are worthy only of great passions.

In 1920 Soutine was in Cagnes when he learned of Modigliani's death. His periods of residence in Cagnes alternated with sojourns in Céret, until his return to Paris, with a considerable number of paintings, at the beginning of 1922. During these years he had worked more frantically than ever, heaping his canvases one upon the other. He is said to have painted approximately 200 works between 1919 and 1922.

Despite the resistance of purchasers, Zborowski's admiration never faltered, and he continued to support Soutine to the extent permitted by his erratic income, occasionally with the assistance of one Netter, another enthusiast. But this almost universal indifference continued until a day toward the end of of 1922, when an American, Dr. Barnes, who had amassed an enormous fortune in the manufacturing of pharmaceutical products (in particular Argyrol), was brought to Zborowski's quarters by a young art dealer named Paul Guillaume. Here Dr. Barnes discovered the unknown artist, and became so enthusiastic about his work that at a single sitting he purchased a large number of canvases for a total price of sixty thousand francs, a sum greatly in excess of the prices then current.

Chana Orloff's story of this event is based on Soutine's description:

«One day, when Soutine came to collect his allowance from Zborowski, he found the dealer extremely excited and wandering from room to room.

« Today we break open the champagne! » Zborowski told him. « I've just sold 75 of your canvases to Dr. Barnes, an American collector. »

«Soutine thought it was a practical joke, and became angry.

« Give me my five francs so I can get out of here! »

« Starting today, » Zborowski replied, « you're going to be paid twenty five francs a day. » And he paid Soutine on the spot.

«Still convinced that it was a joke, but delighted by the windfall, Soutine picked up this incredible sum of money and departed. That evening he went to Montparnasse, where the artists gathered around him to offer their congratulations. But Soutine remained skeptical.

«The next day Zborowski paid a visit to Soutine.

« Barnes wants to meet you. Come with me quickly! »

«Soutine reluctantly dressed and followed Zborowski to his house, where Dr. Barnes was waiting for them.

« . . . He conceived an implacable hatred for Barnes. »

Word of this step upward spread very quickly in Montparnasse, and Soutine abruptly graduated from the role of hapless unfortunate and semiderelict to that of important celebrity. He himself was stunned by what had happened to him so suddenly, and appeared to be dazzled, intoxicated, and disarmed by this completely unhoped-for success. His silk shirts and his suits made by the best tailors became famous, but even when he was traveling in a chauffeured limousine he did not completely lose his hunted look. In 1927 Bing organized Soutine's first one-man exhibition. However, success did not free him from his profound anxiety.

He made increasing demands on his art, to the point that on numerous occasions Zborowski was obliged to trick him out of his canvases before the artist had a chance to destroy them, or even to gather up the torn fragments, which he then gave to a restorer, Jacques, who had become extremely skillful at this work. This was a strange period of inconsistency, in which security resulted in dissatisfaction.

In this connection Jean Leymarie quotes from a letter written to Zborowki in 1923 during one of Soutine's sojourns in Cagnes. In it the artist confesses to this strange discouragement just at a time when life was becoming easy:

«I received the money order. Thank you. I'm sorry I didn't write to you sooner about my work. This is the first time I've been unable to do something. I am depressed and demoralized, which has an influence on me. I have only seven canvases. I'm sorry. I'd like to leave this Cagnes landscape, which I can't bear. I even went for a few days to Cap Martin, where I was thinking of moving. I didn't like it. I had to rub out the canvases I had begun. I am once again at Cagnes, against my will, where instead of landscapes I shall have to do a few wretched still lifes. You can understand my unsettled situation. Can't you advise me about a place because on several occasion I've had the thought of returning to Paris. »

What is the explanation for this lassitude? Perhaps Soutine was chronically unstable, a hypothesis which would seem to be proved by his sudden changes of mood and his fitful friendships. And we should consider above all his nomadic instinct, which nothing could dispel, either materially or spiritually. During the next few years he moved frequently, readily moving in with anyone anywhere. He is known to have had a number of studios in Paris: in the rue du Saint-Gothard (around 1925), where he painted most notably the *Carcass of Beef* series. Somewhat later he was at 9, boulevard Edgar-Quinet, then in the rue de l'Aude, then at Le Blanc, north of Limoges. In 1928 he went to Nice, Châtelguyon, and Bordeaux, thence returning to Paris and the passage Denfert, the avenue d'Orléans, and, probably for a longer period, 18, villa Seurat. Chana Orloff saw him frequently and tamed his unsociability to the point where they became good friends.

Of all these meetings, that with the Castaing family was to be the most permanent and the most favorable for his living conditions. Soutine had become acquainted with these admirers around 1928, and had seen them occasionally in the intervening years, until finally a more stable relationship was established. Soon he was received at their home like a member of the family, and spent increasingly long periods of time with them on their estate at Lèves, near Chartres. Zborowski's death in 1932, coming in conjunction with the economic crisis that had just spread from the United States to Europe, gave the Castaing family an opportunity to strengthen its ties with Soutine and more easily provide him with material support so that he could work without fear of poverty.

His material existence was now more secure, but this did not set his soul at rest, and until the very end his art was to retain the imprint of the years of humiliations and anguish. With much good will some critics can discern phases of greater relaxation in his work, but never the genuine calm of a spirit that has been set at rest.

Soutine more than any other artist helps us to become conscious of the meaning and place of ugliness in art. Hitherto the ugly had been a special preserve, and had played only a limited role in the works of those artists who made use of it; it appears as one facet of their imagination, a series of distorting mirrors in their observation of life. In Goya's work ugliness is the secret face of his torment, which sometimes spills over into reality; in Breughel it is a truculent game tinged with popular farce and spontaneous verve. For Bosch it is an intellectual manner of looking at the world in reverse, while in Grünewald it already approaches a permanent condition. In all of these painters the existence of a less grim version persists.

With Soutine, ugliness is a permanent condition that excludes any other expression. Its presence can no longer be evaded, and its constant affirmation reunites with that abstraction that may be an ideal beauty. In the work of many artists it appears in the form of caricature, and constitutes an act of liberation and a kind of counterproof, the rejoinder to an unduly exclusive submission to the rules of beauty. I remember the illustrations in a turn-of-the-century book on the caricatures of Puvis de Chavannes, in which this apostle of the most purified and most immaterial ideal forms seems to take his revenge for having appeared to ignore the flaws of a society of whose material and spiritual monstrosities he was only too well aware. In Soutine there is no countercurrent in the opposite direction. There is not a single indulgent or tender image, not one affectionate smile in his game of scapegoat, just as there is no lessening of his anxiety, even when circumstances become favorable for him. Ugliness is his domain, anxiety his climate, passion his permanent condition.

At this level, words and feelings acquire a meaning different from the one they have when compared with and counterbalanced against their antonyms in normal life. When thus isolated in its absolute form, ugliness becomes a translation of beauty, also considered as an absolute, a radiant, intransigent beauty that imposes its presence even when one is tempted to reject it. The decomposed flesh of Soutine's lacerated animals is, when all is said and done, more sumptuous, more palpitating with emotion, and more luminous than Gustave Moreau's cascades of gems.

If his sanguinolent animals all have an appearance of the supernatural, it is very probably due to the fact that Soutine consciously or otherwise imparts to them, or suffers the memory of the ritual sacrifices he witnessed in his childhood, and which remained profoundly embedded in his memory, with their atmosphere of religious terror. Basically his entire art bears the imprint of religiosity, a constant confrontation of the human being and his tragic fate with implacable nature. He acts in the capacity of an inspired mystic, and for this reason our judgments on the relative values of objects and our comparisons between better and less good are powerless in the face of his intransigence, which naturally knows of no such gradations. His paintings have the brilliance and intensity of medieval stained glass windows, their vivid colors, their absence of concern for photographic precision of subordinate details, their painful ruthlessness. They must be regarded as mystical windows, not as paintings comparable to other paintings that translate material facts.

Nor can the violence of Soutine's expressionism be judged in relation to a material situation; the most intense works do not always belong to the periods of his greatest misery. Generally speaking, the caricatural figures appear around 1922, the bellhops and page boys around 1930, the tormented birds around 1925 - 26, the skinned animal carcasses around 1925, during periods, that is, in which his material existence was no longer threatened.

An interesting psychological study could be made of the palette utilized in Soutine's paintings and the dominance of certain colors during various periods. In particular, red, the most provocative color and the one that corresponds to his state of constant ecstasy, forms the basis for the largest number of his paintings. There are the red of the skinned carcass and the red stains on the birds offered as a sacrifice, but there is also the red of the choirboys and the bellhops, that of several portraits of women, and that of the gladioli, as lacerating as a scream. Then there is the red in the landscapes of Castres, and that of the pavement in front of Chartres Cathedral. This does not correspond to a factual reality; it expresses an obsession and an exasperation, like the torero's provocation before the bull. Soutine liberates himself from it and luxuriates in it, and his lyricism derives from it a more clarion resonance.

68

Female Nude, 1933
Oil, 18¹/₈" x 10⁵/₈"
Coll. Mr. and Mrs.
Ralph Colin, New York

RETURN FROM SCHOOL AFTER THE STORM, 1939
Oil, 17" x 19½"
Phillips Gallery, Washington, D.C.

CHILDREN ON A ROAD, ca. 1938
Oil, 15⅝" x 12½"
Perls Galleries, New York

71

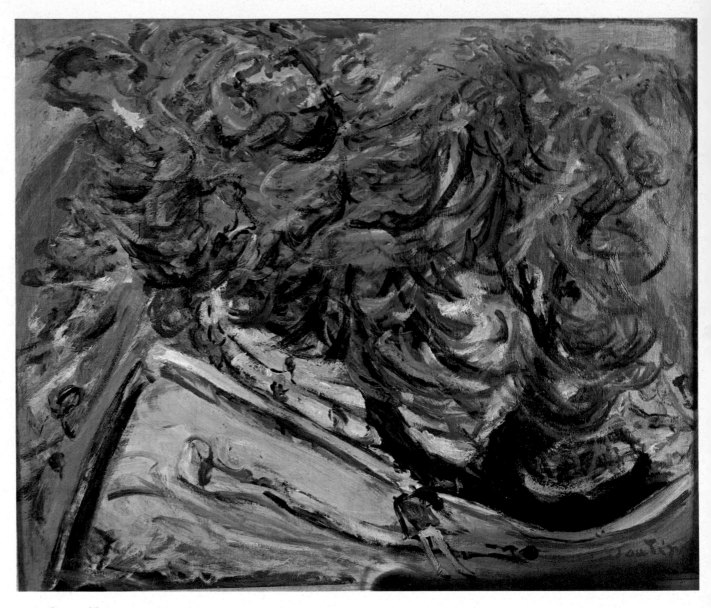

GREEN TREES, 1936
Oil, 23¼" x 28¼" . Private collection

GIRL AT FENCE, 1942
Oil, 33" x 25½" ▷
Coll. Mr. and Mrs. Nathan Cummings, New York

72

WINDY DAY, AUXERRE, 1939
Oil, 19½" x 25⅝"
Phillips Gallery, Washington, D.C.

74

LARGE TREE, 1942, Oil, 34½'' x 29½''. Private collection

FAILURE IN SUCCESS

Once his material existence was no longer such a burden, there was reason to hope that Soutine would achieve some kind of peace. He retained his savage style in depicting interlacing trees battling furiously against the wind, but (was it deliberate?) the red disappeared, and green, its complementary color, reigned supreme, peace contrasted with fury. The change of theme is not an adequate explanation of the change of colors, for amid the entrancing landscapes of the Mediterranean coast Soutine had been unable to escape from his hallucinations or abandon himself to a zest for life and joyful colors.

Along the same line of thought, the colors of his early years are more earthy, and the selection is less clearly affirmed. Increasing individuality in his palette parallels the increasing individuality of his style.

War and the persecution of the Jews now reappeared to feed his all-too-real apprehensions. He succeeded in leaving Paris, after narrowly escaping arrest by the Gestapo in June 1941, but because of various misunderstandings he was unable to reach the United States, despite the efforts of friends to obtain an invitation for him. He settled with his companion, Marie-Berthe Aurenche, in the unoccupied zone, at Champigny-sur-Vende in Touraine, where he was more or less welcomed and tolerated, and became again the hunted man, returning to his nomadic destiny, incapable of putting down roots anywhere.

His stomach ulcer worsened, causing him increasing suffering. In 1943 surgery became an absolute necessity. He was first taken to a nursing home in Chinon, and then transported to Paris, some say in a hearse, to avoid inspection and threats by the authorities. Professor Gosset deemed his case so dangerous, since he had a new hemorrhage and peritonitis set in, that emergency surgery had to be performed. He left Chinon on August 6, 1943, arrived in Paris on the 8th, and died on August 9, at six o'clock in the morning.

To the very end his life there was a constant misunderstanding between what was and what he expected, between a soul in search of the absolute and one unable to see those events that occurred to assuage him and fulfill his expectations. His relationships with those who approached him are typical of this irrevocable fate, and are therefore somewhat ambiguous, probably because of his self-doubts and that blend of pride and timidity which gave him the appearance of a frequently suspicious, irritable human being. Violent clashes marked his friendship with Modigliani; Zborowski's devotion did not always forestall conflict, and the hospitality of the Castaing family was not always made to extend easily.

Soutine's relationships with women were also full of hesitations and uncertainties. There can be no question of the devotion of Paulette Jourdain, whom Zborowski had made available to him as an assistant and model around 1925 in the studio in the rue Saint-Gothard, and who poured fresh blood over the series of pictures of game and carcasses he was then painting. We have little information concerning his liaison with the Polish woman Deborah Melnik, except that in 1925 she gave birth to a daughter who bore a strong resemblance to Soutine, but whom he did not recognize. There was also the faithful presence of Madame Gerda Groth, whom he called Mademoiselle Garde, and who because of her German nationality was among the victims of the famous roundup of 1940 at the Hiver velodrome, whence she was evacuated to the concentration camp at Gurs. Lastly, there was Marie-Berthe Aurenche, the touching companion of his last days. But despite their evident devotion to him, none of these women seems to have brought him serenity.

The comparison with van Gogh continues to assert itself, in Soutine's unsatisfactory love affairs and erratic friendships as in his flamboyant painting. For too long he had known Lady Poverty, and she had become his companion and his accomplice; she had become flesh of his flesh, and nothing could separate them. He was impregnated with the monstrous frenzy born of their embrace, and did not even attempt to escape from those prodigious couplings that were his way of life until the very end.

His trees writhe in the wind because the hurricane is his climate and his indispensable nourishment; they twist their disheveled foliage under a cataclysmic sky, just as van Gogh's cypresses burst into flame under the burning sun. Both artists paint their sumptuous despairs and their insatiable rages in shining colors. Disorder is their order, the exceptional is their moderation, and it is impossible to imagine what could be their peace. Soutine, who sold everything he painted, was as miserable and felt as isolated as van Gogh, who sold nothing and received only subsidies from his brother. The refuge of the Castaing family was the equivalent of the one offered by Dr. Gachet; it did not fill this void, which could not be filled because it is of the essence of these persons destined to an inescapable fate. The tardy operation that led to Soutine's death corresponds to van Gogh's suicide, and neither man, despite appearances, was free to choose his drama.

We are even tempted to believe that fate, in order to eliminate any misunderstanding, repeated the course of events with Soutine (who was born a short time after van Gogh's death), as if she wished to begin anew in accordance with an analogous psychological and physical process, and to demonstrate that financial success would have changed nothing, since it would inevitably have led to the same dramatic impasse and the same solitude, and that this is the price that had to be paid for a certain kind of grandeur.

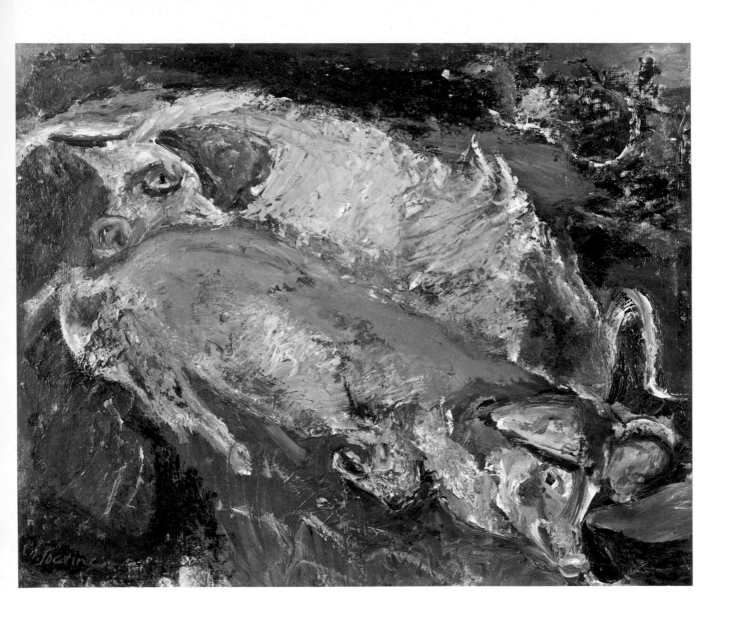

THE PIGS, 1942
Oil, 18¾" x 23"
Musée d'Art Moderne de la Ville de Paris

BIOGRAPHY

1893. Chaim Soutine is born in Belorussia, near Minsk, the tenth child in a large family. His father, a tailor, decides that his son will become a craftsman. By the age of fourteen, Chaim feels the need for freedom from his family and goes to Minsk, capital of Belorussia, where he becomes acquainted with Michael Kikoïne. The two young men become close friends, and attend drawing classes together, while Soutine is earning his living as an assistant to a photographer in the city.

1910. Soutine registers at art school in Vilna.

1912. Soutine, like all the young artists of his day, is attracted to Paris. He arrives there in 1912 and joins his friend Kikoïne at La Ruche, in the 15th *arrondissement*. Goes to live with Kikoïne. Registers at the Ecole des Beaux-Arts, and also studies for a time at Cormon's studio.

1914. When the war breaks out, Soutine and Kikoïne volunteer for service in the French army. Soutine becomes acquainted with Modigliani at the Cité Falguière, where he is then living.

1916. Soutine paints his first still lifes. Becomes acquainted with Leopold Zborowski, a well-known art dealer who is selling Modigliani's works. Zborowski handles Soutine's paintings from this time on.

1918. Toward the end of the war, Soutine goes to the south of France for the first time; he and Modigliani spend some time in Vence. Foreigners are not welcome in the town, and Soutine is accused, without cause and without proof, of making anti-French remarks. He leaves Vence, and goes to Cagnes and Céret.

1920. Death of Modigliani; Soutine learns the news of his death at Cagnes. He returns to Céret, where he remains until 1922. The painter Emile Lejeune commissions his series of « Men Praying. » Soutine returns to Paris with a large number of paintings. At the end of 1922, Dr. Barnes, an American pharmacist and art collector, sees Soutine's paintings at Zborowski's home and purchases some 100 canvases for his home in Merion, near Philadelphia.

1925. A difficult period for Soutine. He has been painting landscapes in the south of France, and is looking for new themes: still lifes with fowl and game, sides of beef that he orders from the Villette slaughterhouses. He is haunted by Rembrandt's *Carcass of Beef.*

1926. Soutine takes up residence in Paris with Paulette Jourdain, with whom he has become acquainted through Zborowski. Remains in Paris until 1928. Paints the series of communicants, pastry cooks, and still lifes on tables.

1927. In June, first Soutine exhibition in Paris, organized by Henri Bing. Soutine becomes better acquainted with the Castaing family, whom he had met briefly a short time before. Paints the portrait of Madeleine Castaing and valet series. Divides his time between the south of France and the spas in the Massif Central, where he meets the Castaing family regularly.

1929. In Bordeaux, he makes the acquaintance of Elie Faure, who publishes a small book on Soutine. The artist returns to Vence, and paints his series of trees.

1930. Soutine returns to Paris; becomes increasingly intimate with the Castaing family, who invite him to their estate at Chartres.

1932. Death of Leopold Zborowski. The Castaings undertake to support Soutine.

1935. First major Soutine exhibition in the United States, at the Chicago Art Club. A friend gives him the use of a small private house in Paris.

1937. Soutine moves into the Villa Seurat in the Alésia area of Paris. Soutine exhibition at the Leicester Gallery in London. In Montparnasse, he becomes acquainted with Gerda Groth, whom he is to call Mademoiselle Garde. She acts as his housekeeper and accompanies him on his travels.

1939. Outbreak of the war. Soutine and Mademoiselle Garde are staying in a little village called Civry, some miles southeast of Paris, where they are regarded as refugees. Soutine volunteers for a second time for the French army, but is rejected for reasons of health. He stays in the village and paints his poplar series. A Soutine exhibition is organized in New York.

1940. In May Mademoiselle Garde is deported by the Germans. Soutine leaves Civry in 1941 and moves into a small hotel in Paris. The roundups have begun. He becomes acquainted with Marie-Berthe Aurenche, ex-wife of Max Ernst; she takes care of him. Feeling that he is in danger, she takes him to some friends who live along the road to Versailles. Thanks to a new friend, M. Moulin, a veterinarian and the mayor of a town in the department of Indre-et-Loire, a new refuge is found for Soutine, accompanied by Marie-Berthe Aurenche, at Champigny, near Chinon. Soutine works in a studio on the road to Chinon, and leads a quiet, retired life, far from his coreligionists.

1943. Soutine, whose health has never been good, is suffering with increasing frequency from stomach problems. In 1943 he is taken to the hospital in Chinon. An operation is urgently necessary, but Marie-Berthe Aurenche opposes it and has him taken to Paris in an ambulance. Precautions must be taken to protect Soutine from police persecution. The ambulance makes a detour through Normandy. The dying painter arrives in Paris on August 8. Operated on for a perforated ulcer, he dies one day later, on August 9, 1943.

BIBLIOGRAPHY

BOOKS ILLUSTRATED BY SOUTINE

The following list contains only works devoted exclusively to Soutine. In addition, the numerous articles published in various magazines may usefully be consulted, as well chapters on Soutine in works on the history of art in the twentieth century, and prefaces to the catalogues of his exhibitions.

A. BARNES, *Soutine* (Les Arts à Paris). November 1944.

M. CASTAING et J. LEYMARIE, *Soutin* (Bibliothèque des Arts). Paris, 1963.

R. COGNIAT, *Soutine* (Editions du Chêne). Paris, 1945.

R. COGNIAT, *Soutine*, Trésors de la Peinture (Skira). Geneva, 1952.

ELIE FAURE, *Soutine*, Les Artistes Nouveaux (Crès). 1929.

WALDEMAR GEORGE, *Soutine*, Collection Artistes Juifs (Editions le Triangle). 1928.

WALDEMAR GEORGE, *Soutine* (Editions Art et Style). 1959.

H. SEROUYA, *Soutine* (Hachette). 1961.

SZITTYA, *Soutine et Son Temps* (Bibliothèque des Arts). 1955.

PIERRE COURTHION, *Soutine* (Edita-Denoël). 1972.

PRINCIPAL EXHIBITIONS OF SOUTINE'S WORKS

1927. Paris, Galerie Bing. June

1930. Paris, Théâtre Pigalle

1935. Chicago, Art Club. December

1936. New York, Valentine Gallery. February

1936. New York, Cornelius J. Sullivan Gallery. February-March

1937. New York, Cornelius J. Sullivan Gallery. March-April

1937. New York, Valentine Gallery. May

1937. London, Leicester Galleries. April

1937. Paris, Petit Palais. June-October

1938. London, Storran Gallery. November

1939. New York, Valentine Gallery. March-April

1940. New York, Carrol Carstayrs Gallery. April-May

1943. Washington, D.C., Phillips Gallery. January-February

1943. New York, Bignou Gallery. March-April

1944. New York, Niveau Gallery. October-November

1944. Paris, Salon d'Automne.

1945. Paris, Galerie de France. January-February

1945. Boston, Institute of Modern Art. January-February

1947. London, Gimpel Fils. April-May

1947. Paris, Galerie Zack. November-December

1949. New York, Van Diem Lilienfeld Galleries. January

1950. 1951. New York, Museum of Modern Art. October-January

1952. Venice, Biennale

1953. New York, Perls Galleries. November-December

1956. Paris, Maison de la Pensée Française. March-April

1959. Paris, Galerie Charpentier

1963. London, Tate Gallery. September-November

1966. Paris, Orangerie des Tuileries

1966. New York, Perls Galleries. November-December

1968. Los Angeles. County Museum of Art

1968. Jerusalem. Museum of Israel

1973. New York, Marlborough Gallery. October-November

ILLUSTRATIONS